MAGICAL PET VET

THE UNICORN WITH THE CANDY CORN HORN

By Jason M. Burns
Illustrated by Renata García
Colors by Larh Ilustrador

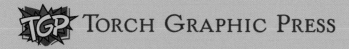

Published in the United States of America by Cherry Lake Publishing Group

Ann Arbor, Michigan

www.cherrylakepublishing.com

Reading Adviser: Beth Walker Gambro, MS, Ed., Reading Consultant, Yorkville, IL

Book Designer: Jason M. Burns

Torch Graphic Press is an imprint of Cherry Lake Publishing Group.

Library of Congress Cataloging-in-Publication Data has been filed and is available at catalog.loc.gov

Cherry Lake Publishing Group would like to acknowledge the work of the Partnership for 21st Century Learning, a Network of Battelle for Kids.

Please visit http://www.battelleforkids.org/networks/p21 for more information.

Printed in the United States of America

Corporate Graphics

Note from publisher: Websites change regularly, and their future contents are outside of our control. Supervise children when conducting any recommended online searches for extended learning opportunities.

TABLE OF CONTENTS

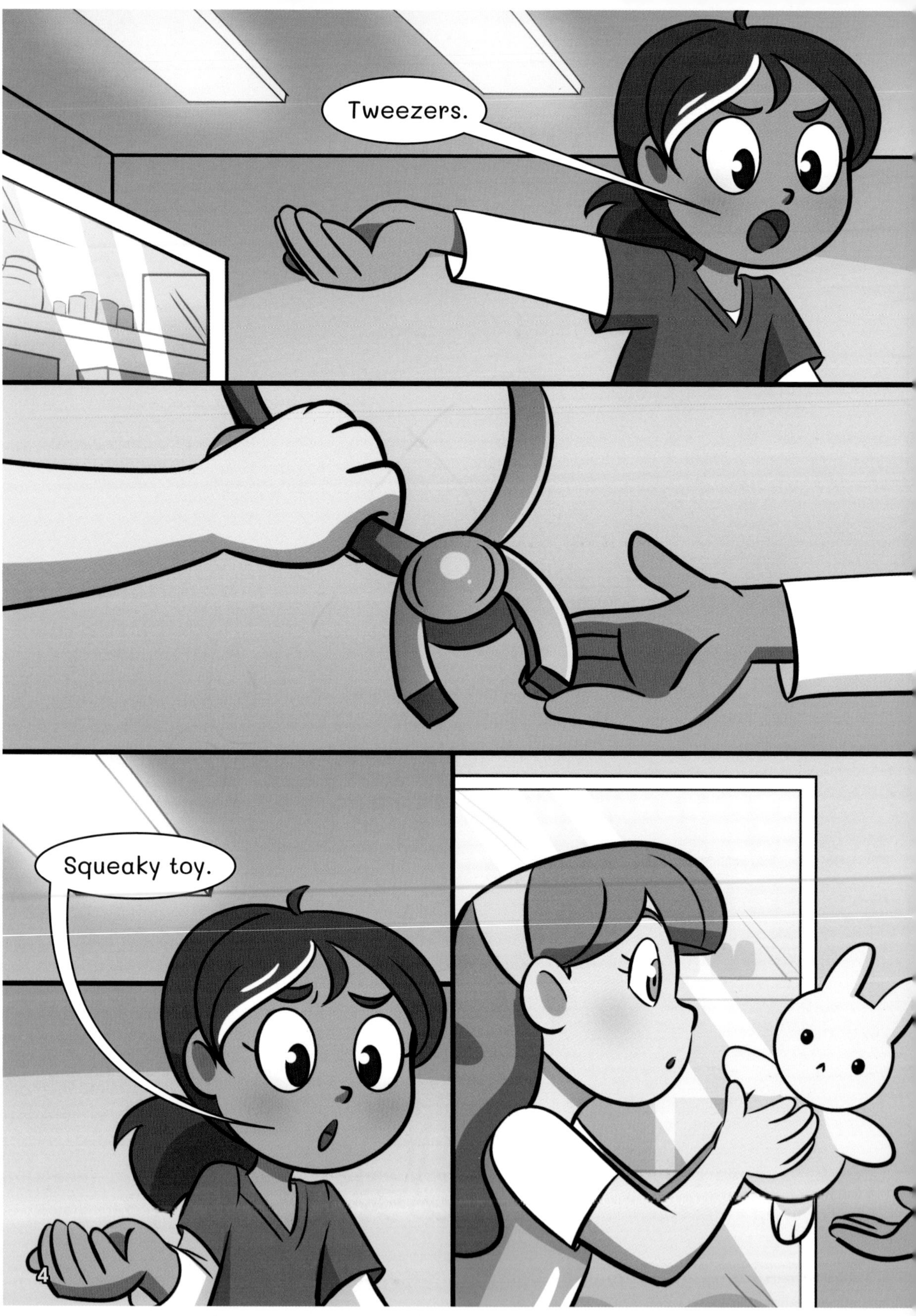
Tweezers.
Squeaky toy.

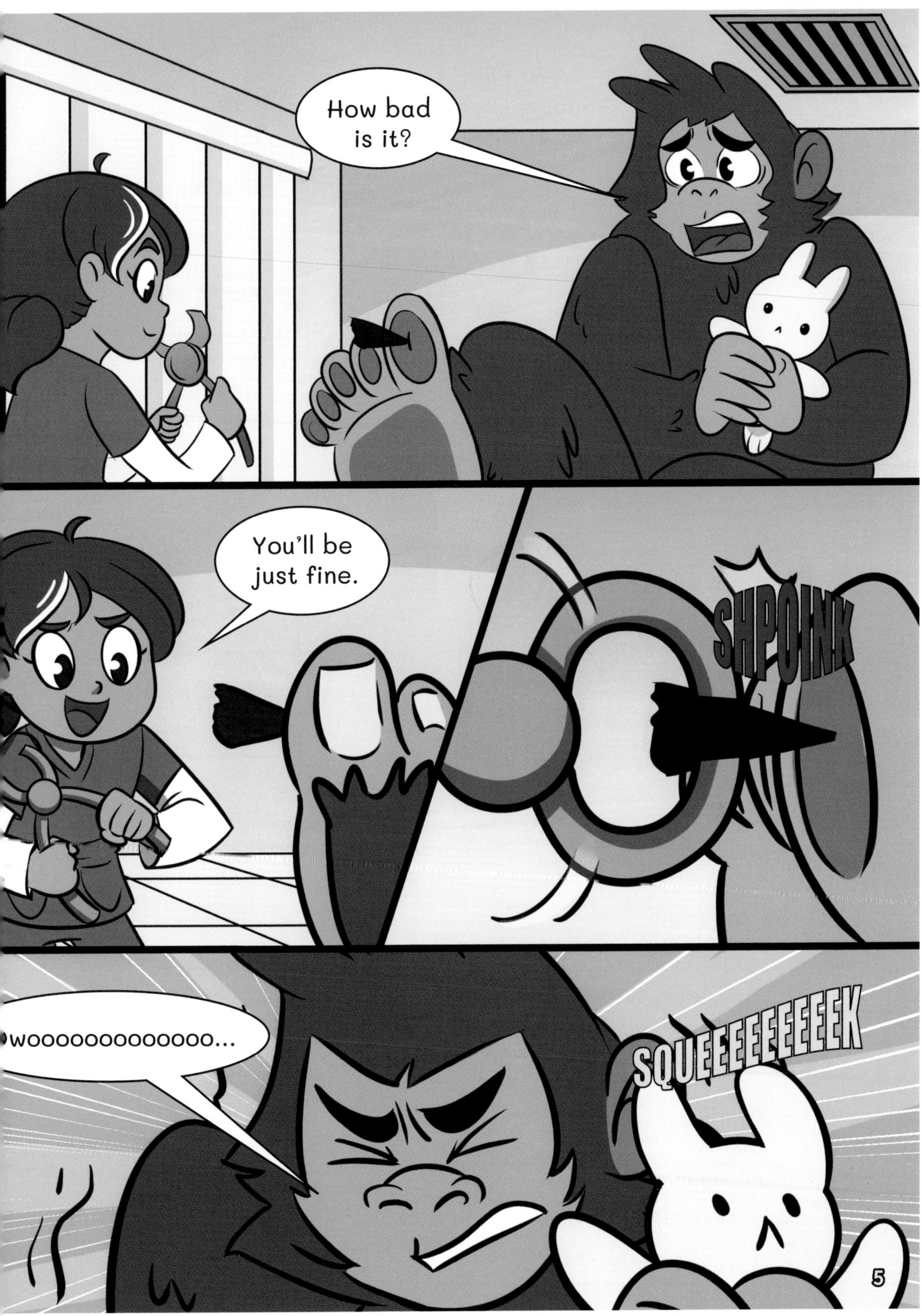
How bad is it?
You'll be just fine.
SHPOINK
WOOOOOOOOOOOOOO...
SQUEEEEEEEEEEK

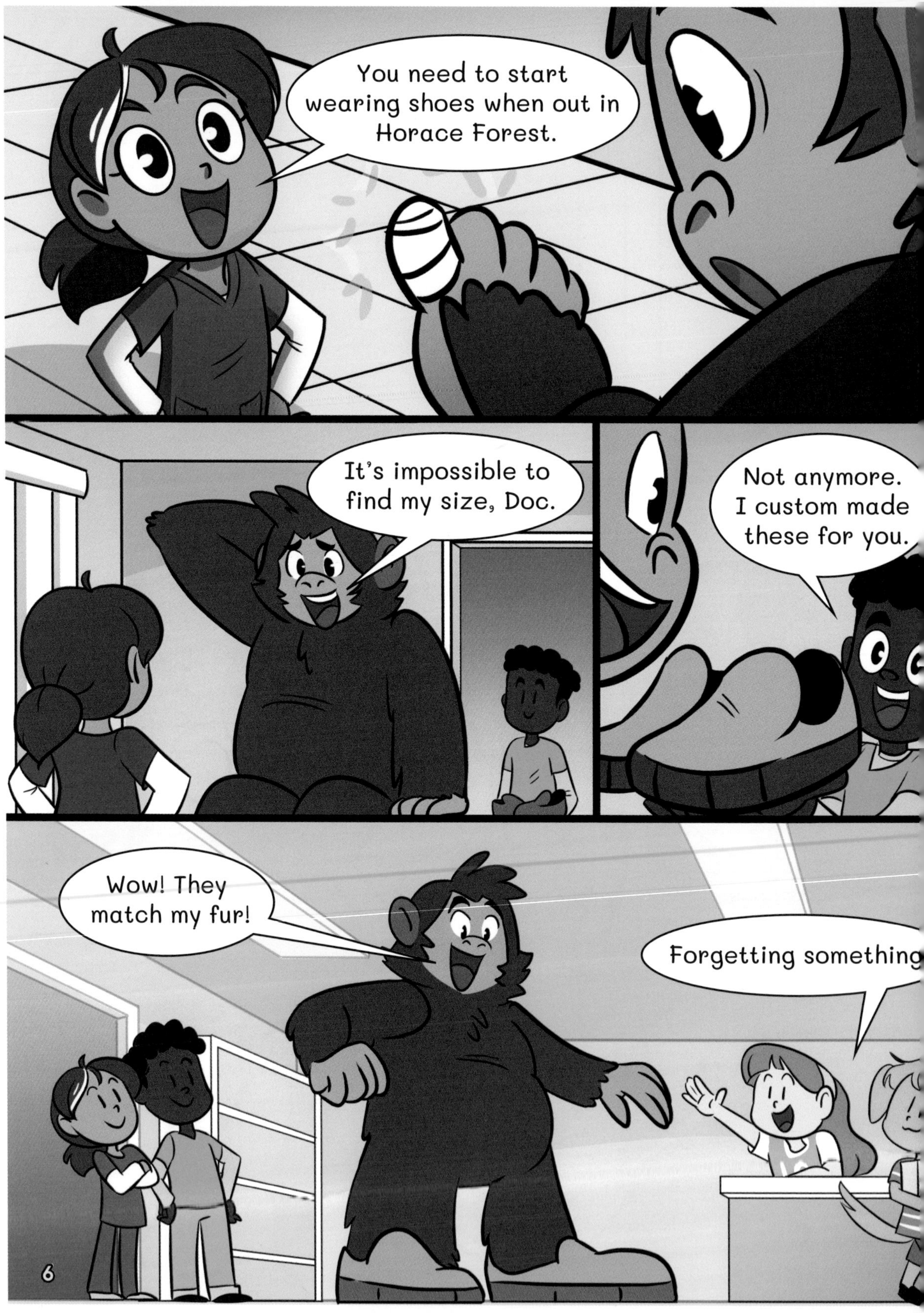

You need to start wearing shoes when out in Horace Forest.
It's impossible to find my size, Doc.
Not anymore. I custom made these for you.
Wow! They match my fur!
Forgetting something

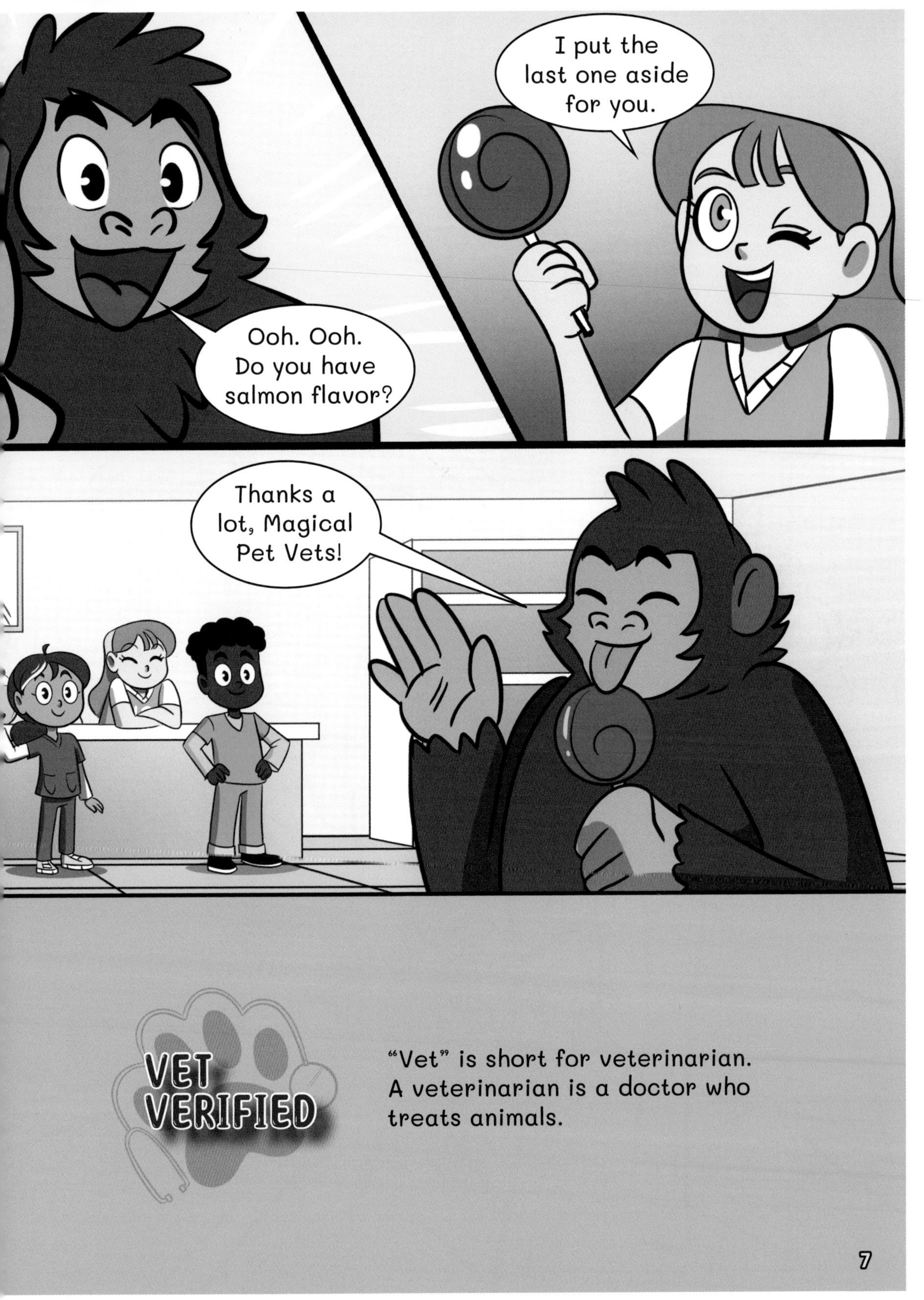
Ooh. Ooh. Do you have salmon flavor?
I put the last one aside for you.
Thanks a lot, Magical Pet Vets!

VET VERIFIED

"Vet" is short for veterinarian. A veterinarian is a doctor who treats animals.

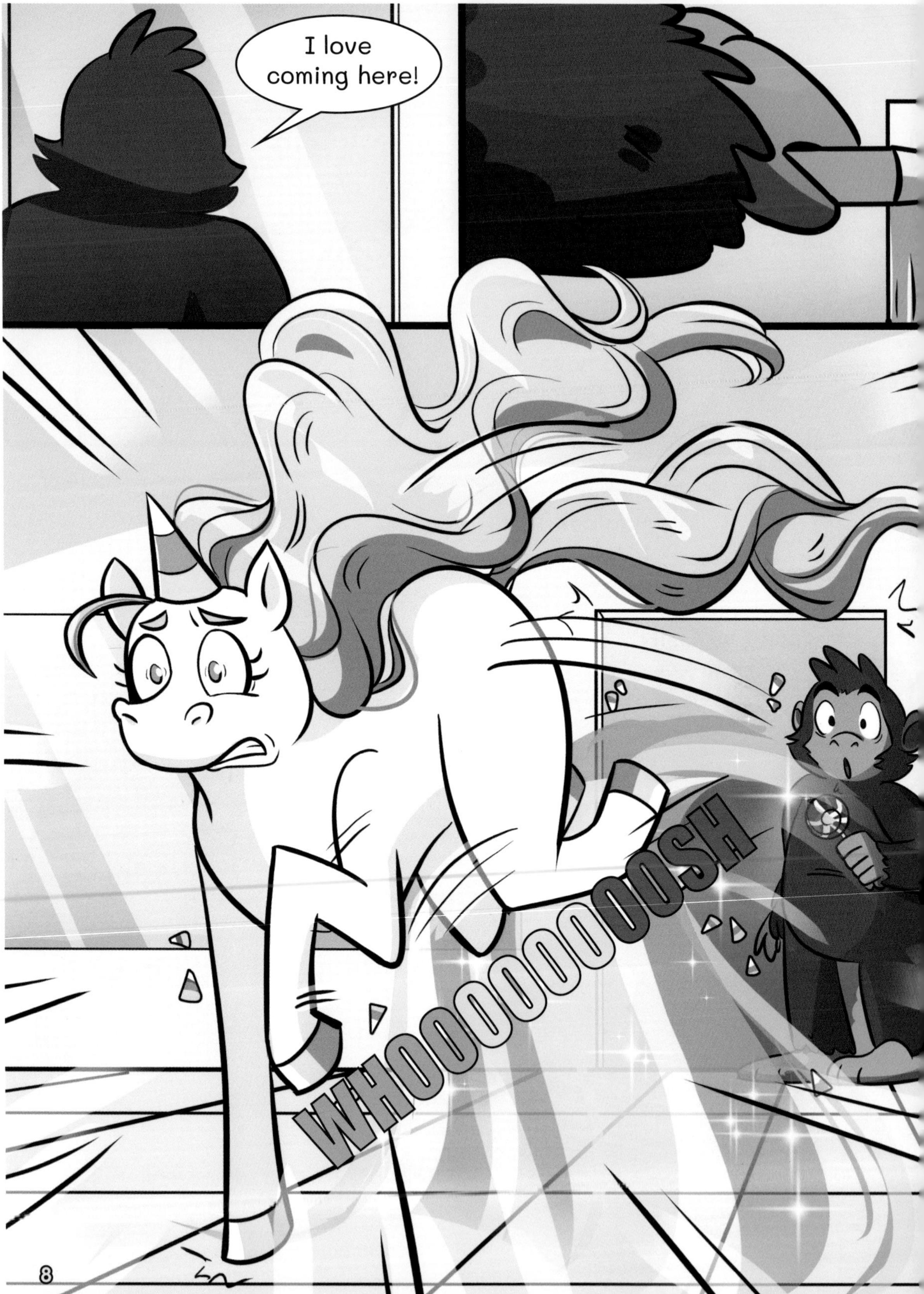
I love coming here!
WHOOOOOOOOOSH

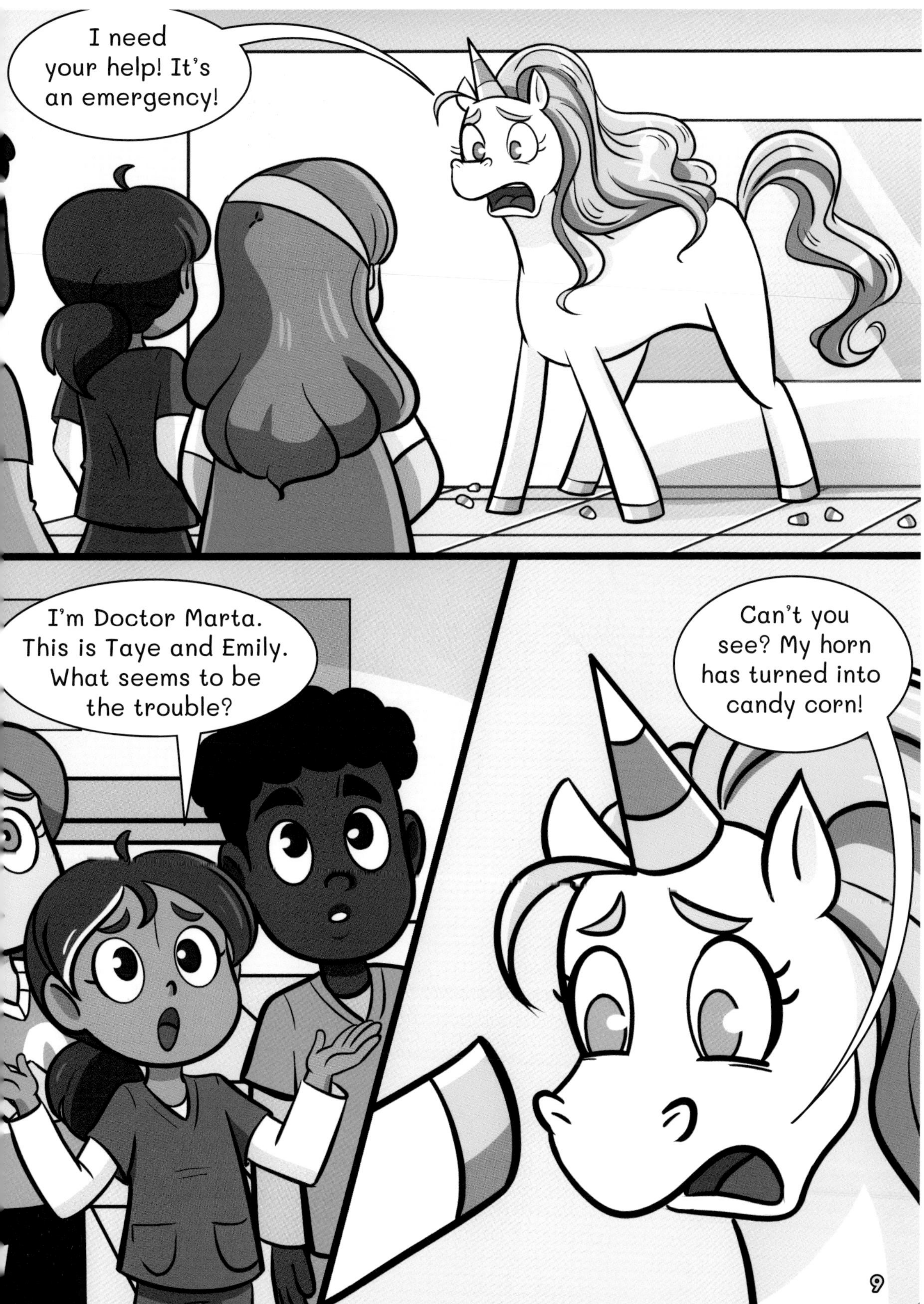
I need your help! It's an emergency!
I'm Doctor Marta. This is Taye and Emily. What seems to be the trouble?
Can't you see? My horn has turned into candy corn!

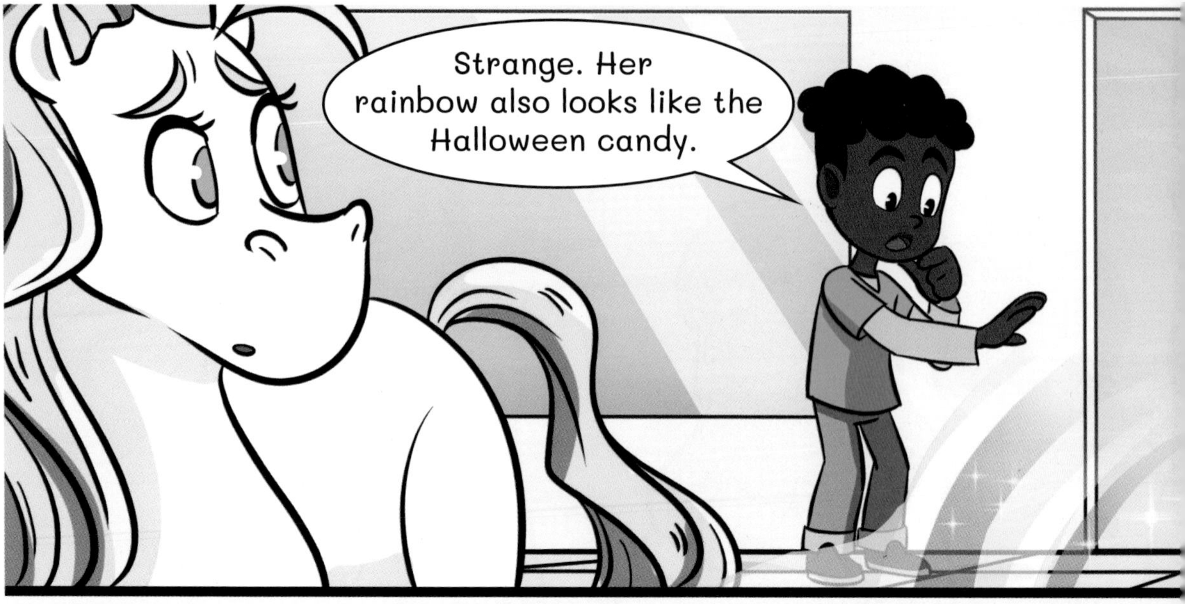
Strange. Her rainbow also looks like the Halloween candy.

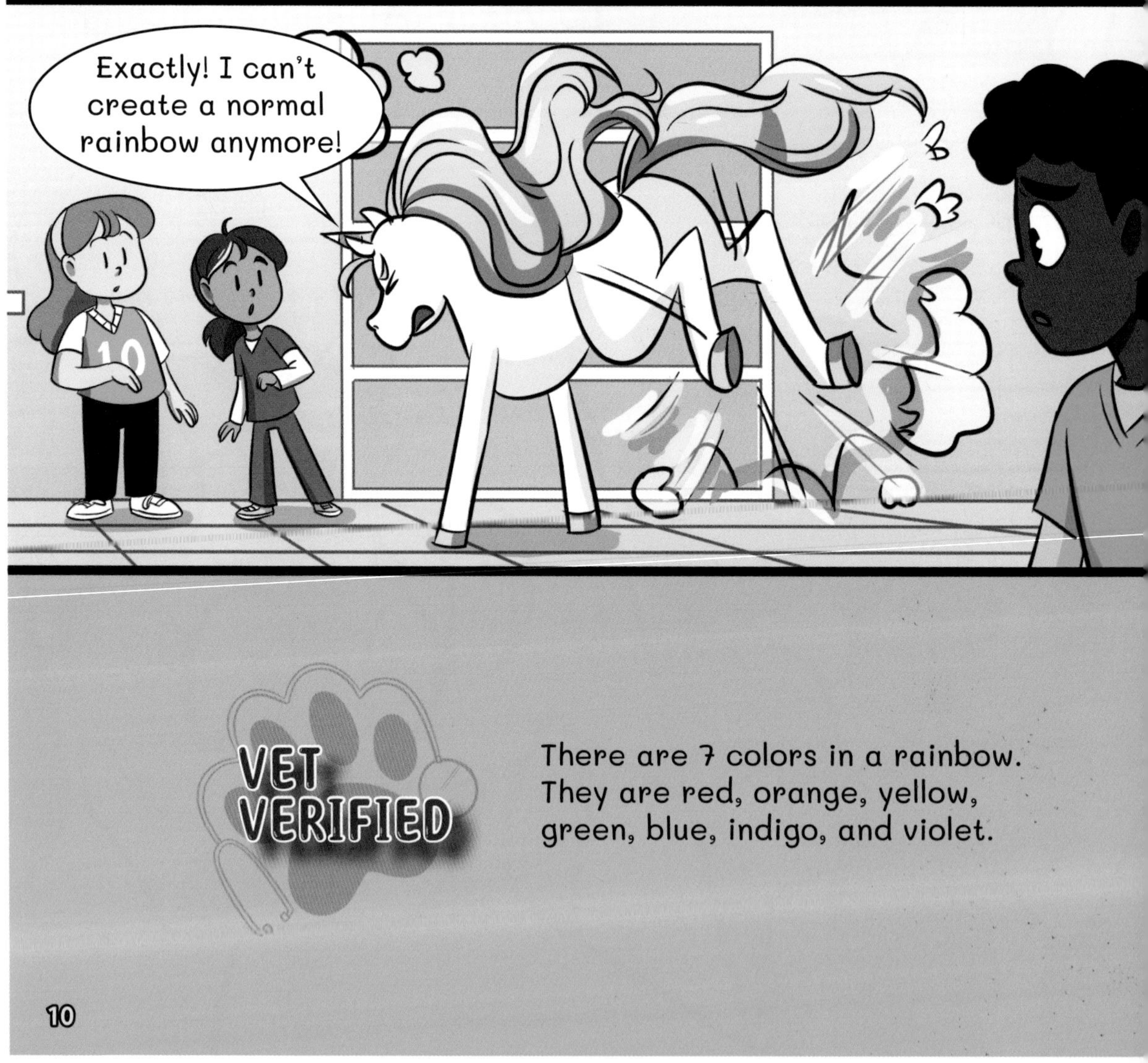
Exactly! I can't create a normal rainbow anymore!

VET VERIFIED

There are 7 colors in a rainbow. They are red, orange, yellow, green, blue, indigo, and violet.

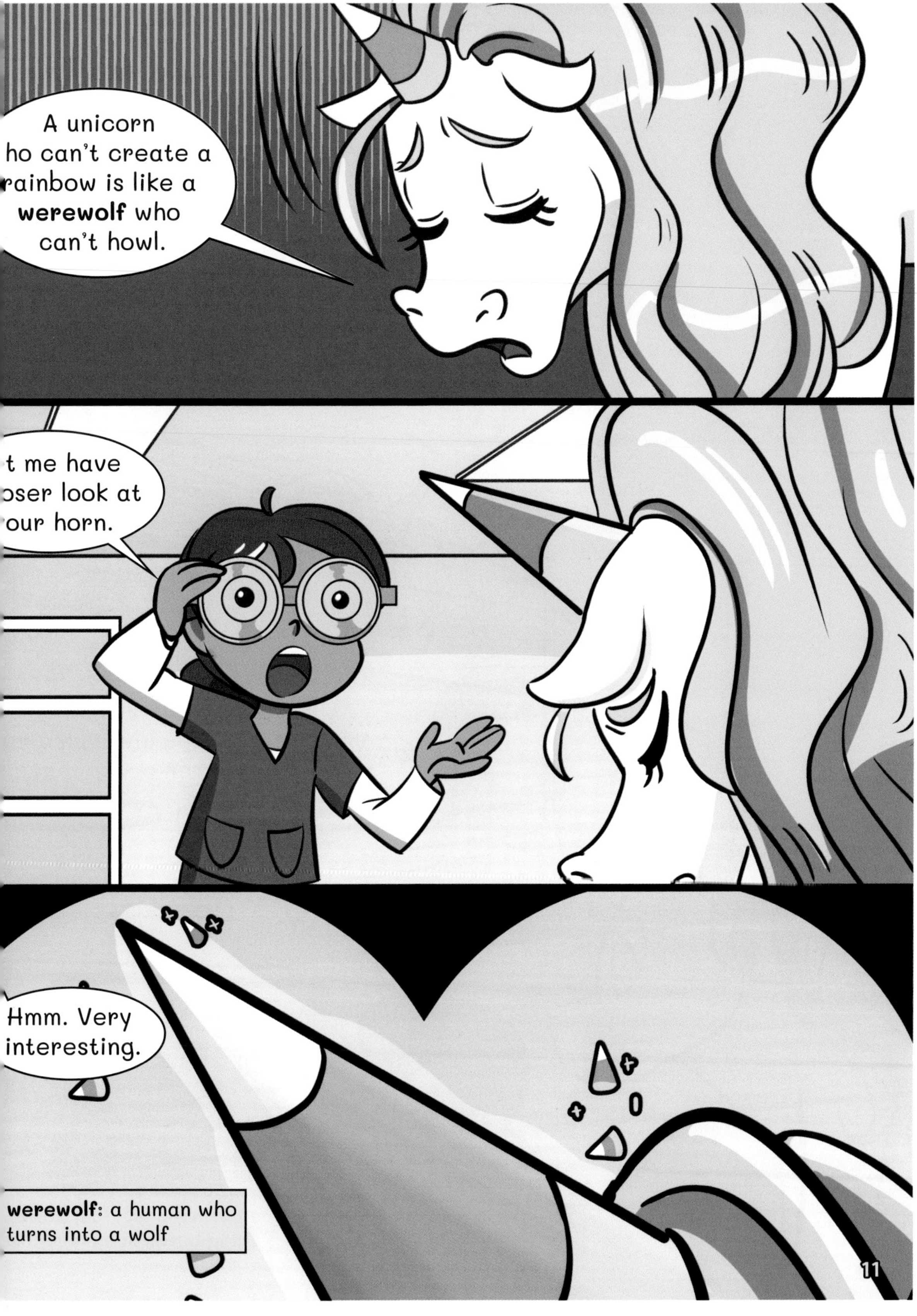
A unicorn ho can't create a rainbow is like a **werewolf** who can't howl.
t me have oser look at our horn.
Hmm. Very interesting.
werewolf: a human who turns into a wolf

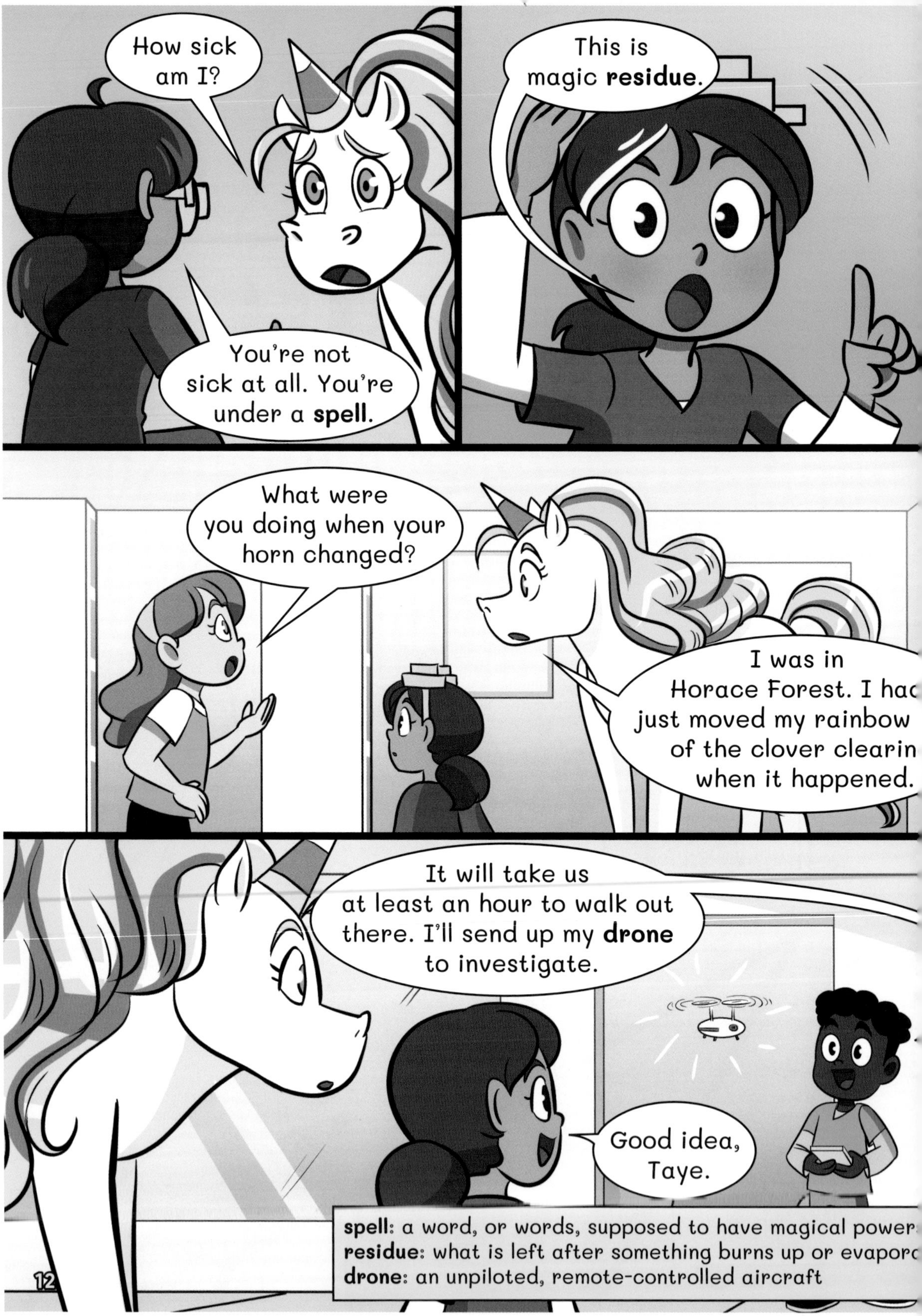
How sick am I?
You're not sick at all. You're under a **spell**.
This is magic **residue**.
What were you doing when your horn changed?
I was in Horace Forest. I had just moved my rainbow of the clover clearin when it happened.
It will take us at least an hour to walk out there. I'll send up my **drone** to investigate.
Good idea, Taye.
spell: a word, or words, supposed to have magical power
residue: what is left after something burns up or evapor
drone: an unpiloted, remote-controlled aircraft

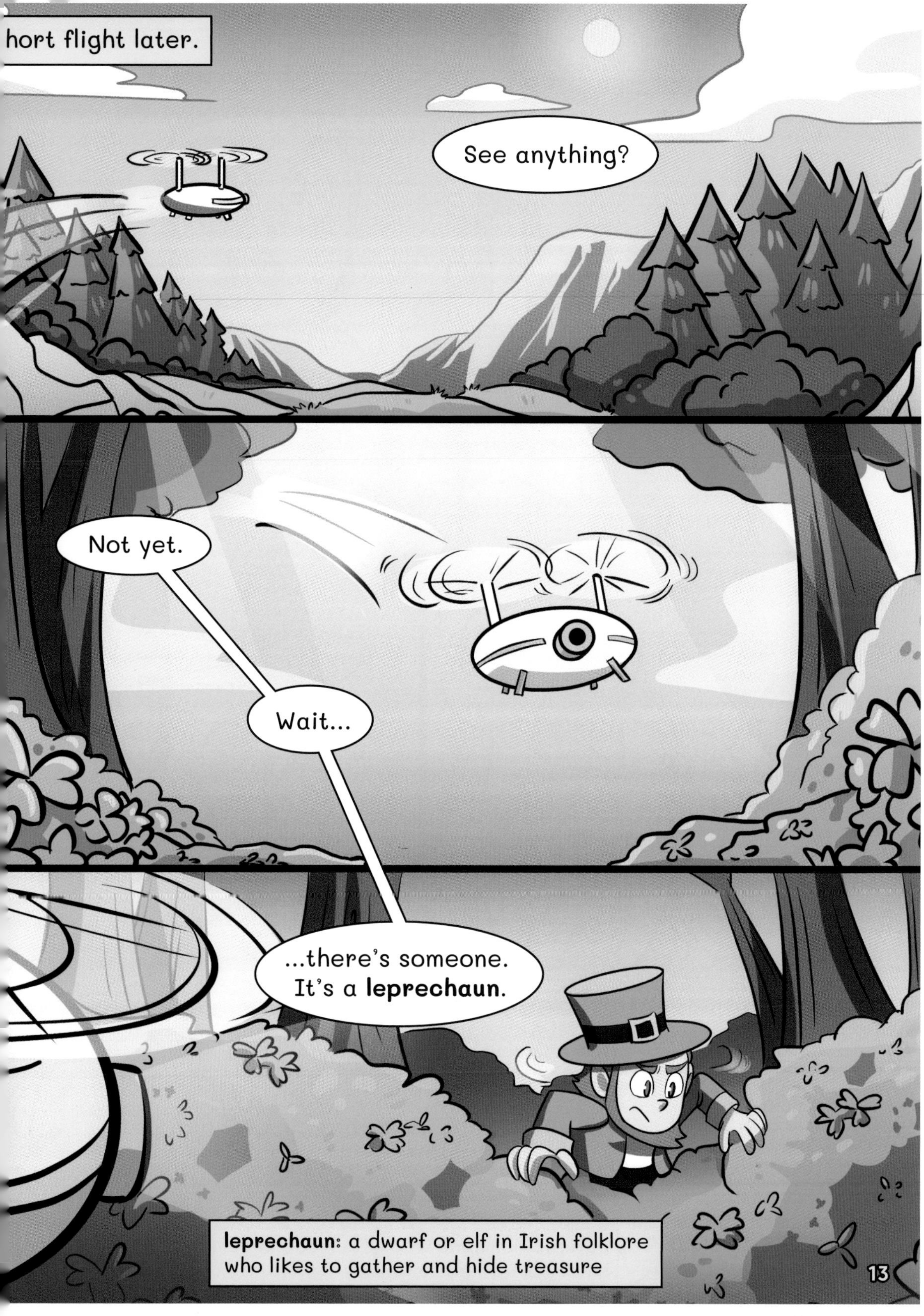

hort flight later.
See anything?
Not yet.
Wait...
...there's someone. It's a **leprechaun**.
leprechaun: a dwarf or elf in Irish folklore who likes to gather and hide treasure

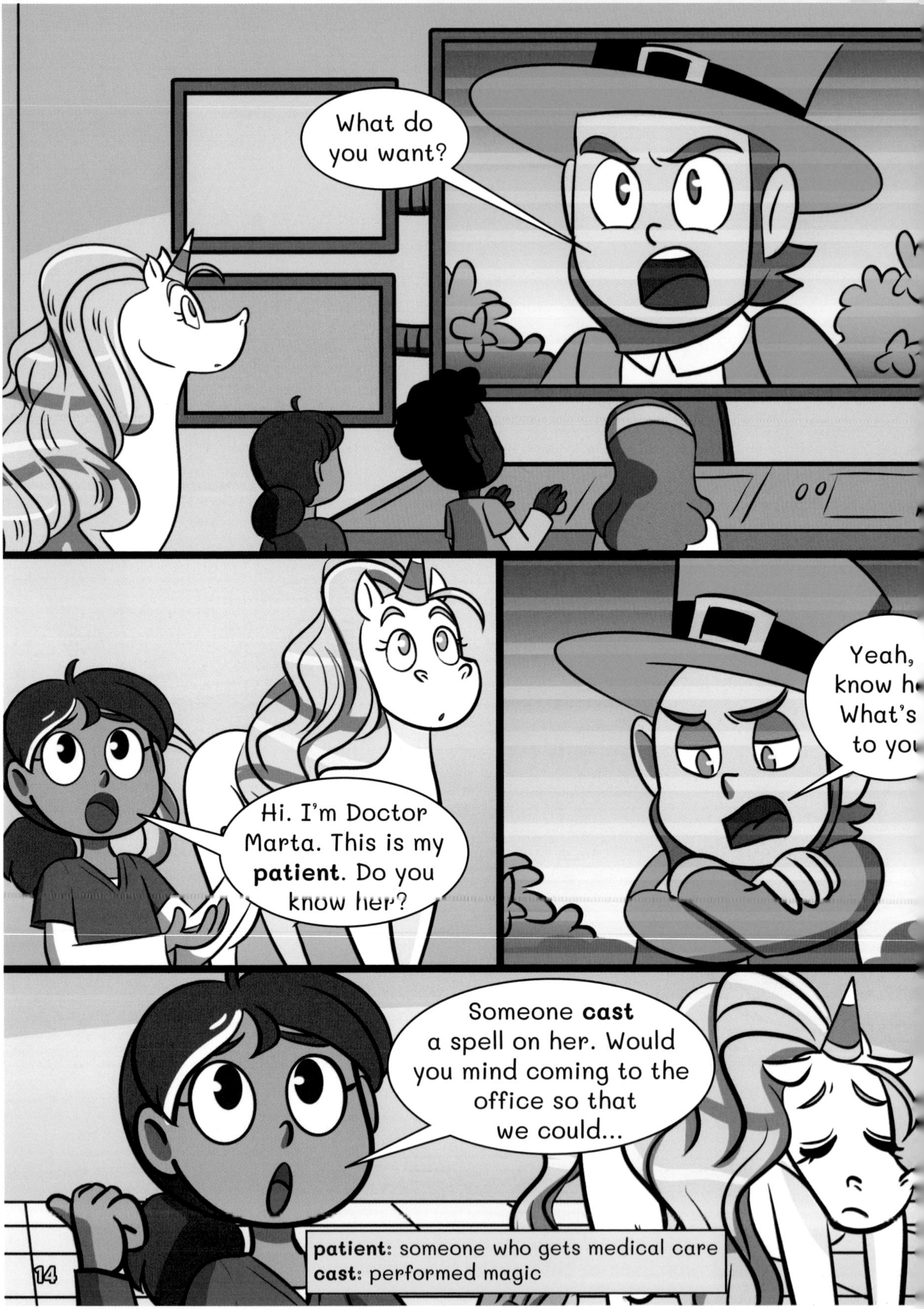
What do you want?
Hi. I'm Doctor Marta. This is my **patient**. Do you know her?
Yeah,
know h
What's
to yo
Someone **cast** a spell on her. Would you mind coming to the office so that we could...

patient: someone who gets medical care
cast: performed magic

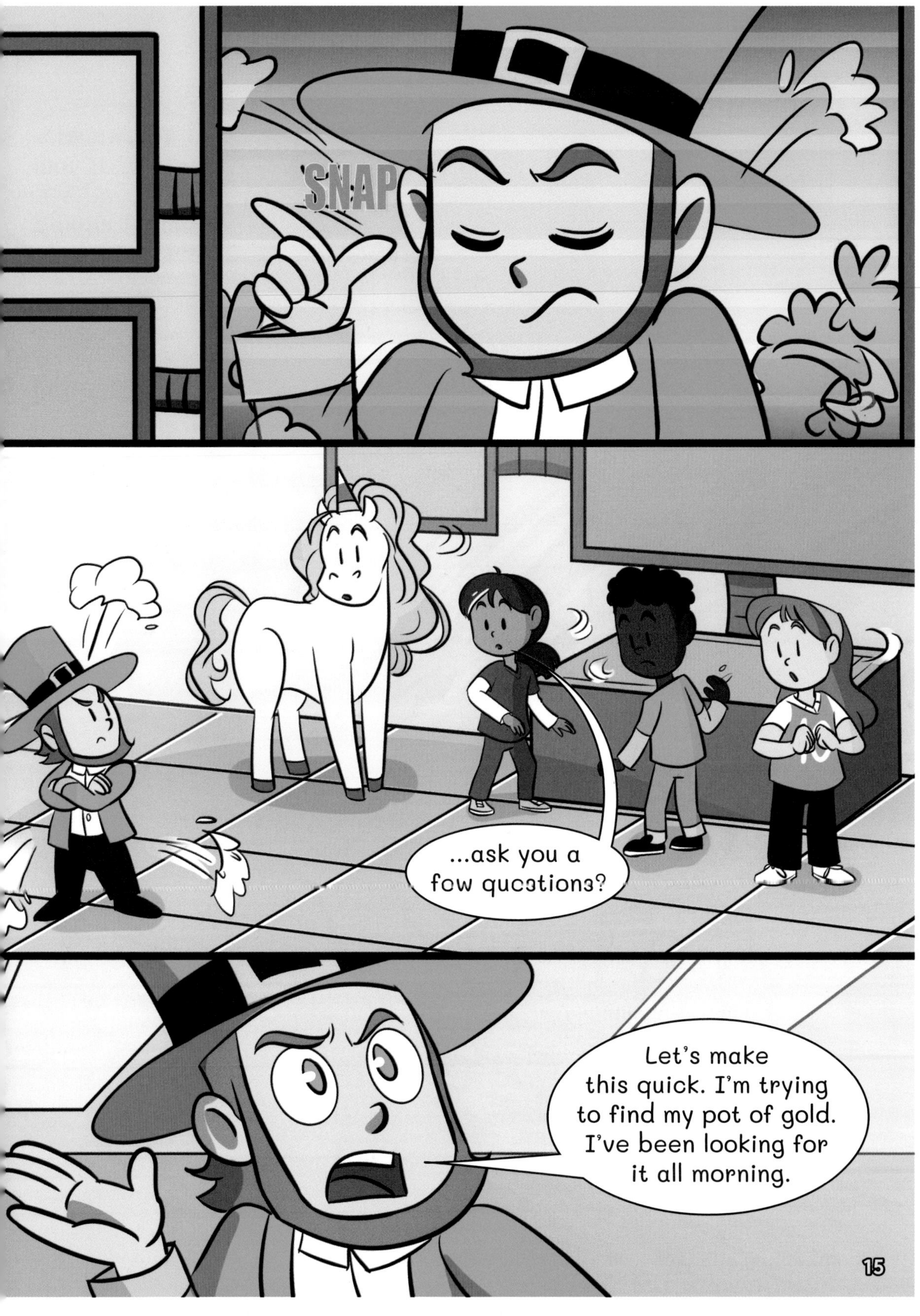
SNAP
...ask you a few questions?
Let's make this quick. I'm trying to find my pot of gold. I've been looking for it all morning.

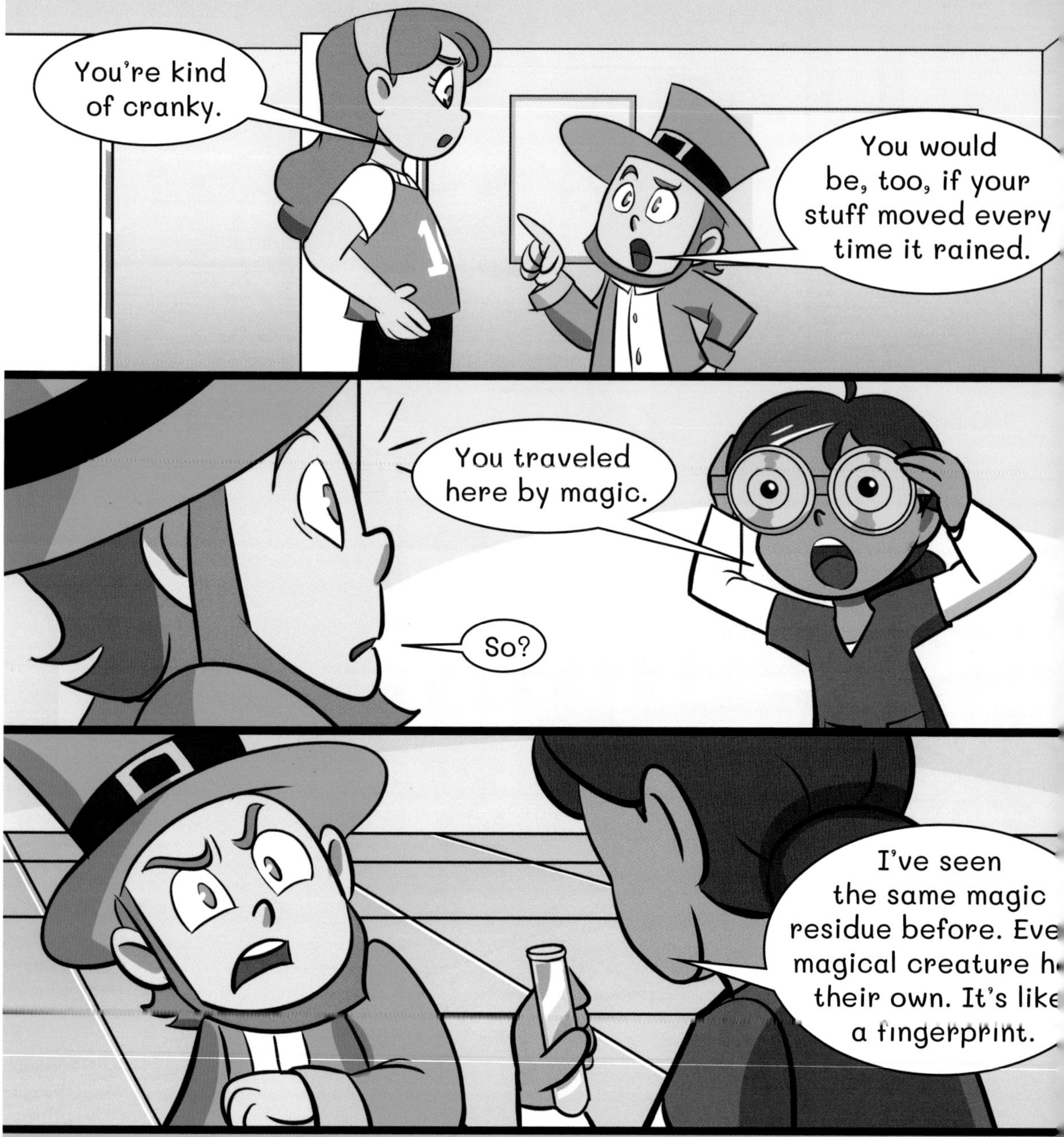
You're kind of cranky.
You would be, too, if your stuff moved every time it rained.
You traveled here by magic.
So?
I've seen the same magic residue before. Eve
magical creature h
their own. It's like
a fingerprint.

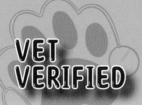

VET VERIFIED

No two people have the same fingerprints. Even identical twins will have different fingerprints.

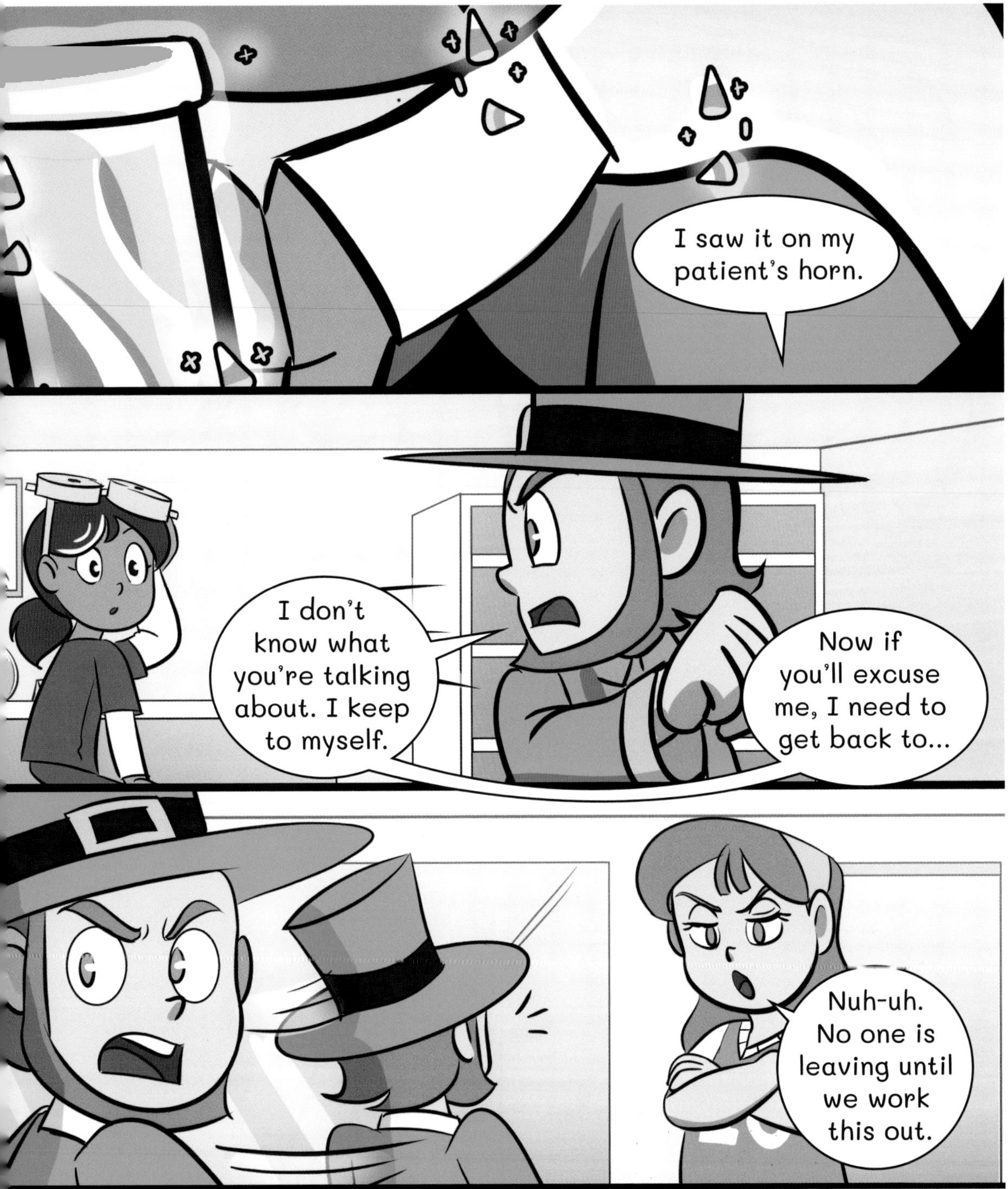
I saw it on my patient's horn.
I don't know what you're talking about. I keep to myself.
Now if you'll excuse me, I need to get back to...
Nuh-uh. No one is leaving until we work this out.

UNLEASHING UNDERSTANDING

It's important to solve conflicts and misunderstandings. Talking things out leads to healthier relationships with family and friends.

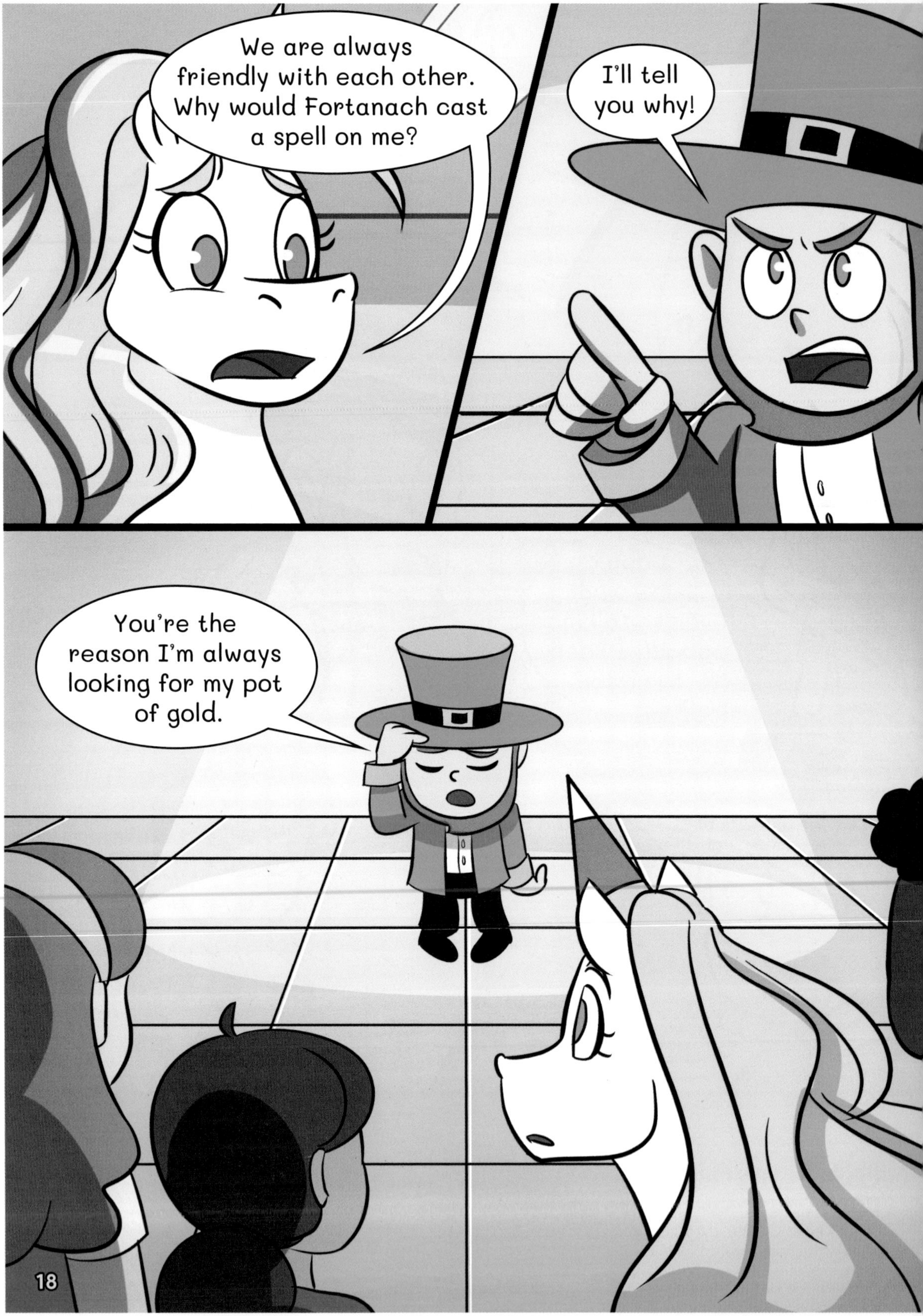
We are always friendly with each other. Why would Fortanach cast a spell on me?
I'll tell you why!
You're the reason I'm always looking for my pot of gold.

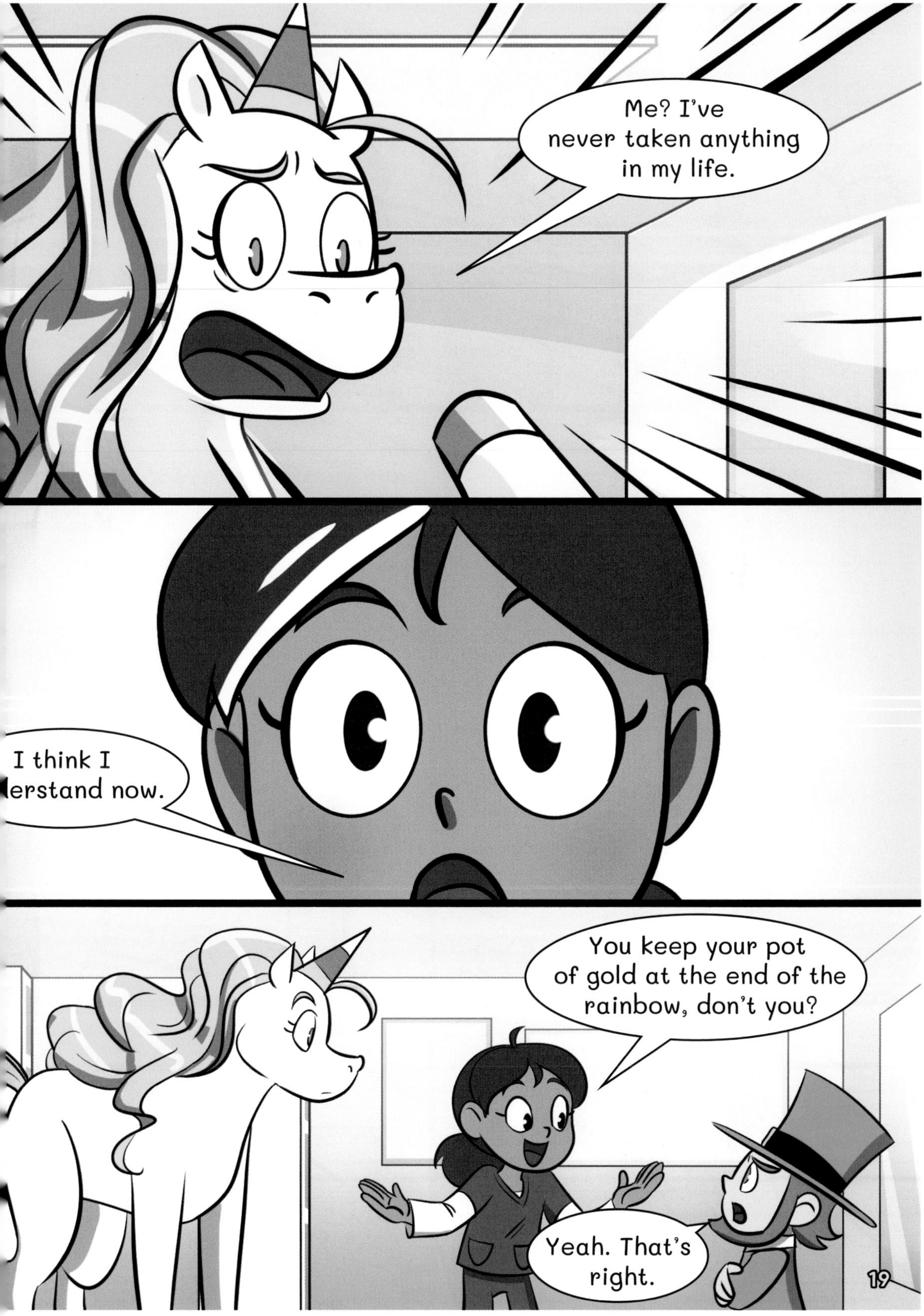
Me? I've never taken anything in my life.
I think I erstand now.
You keep your pot of gold at the end of the rainbow, don't you?
Yeah. That's right.

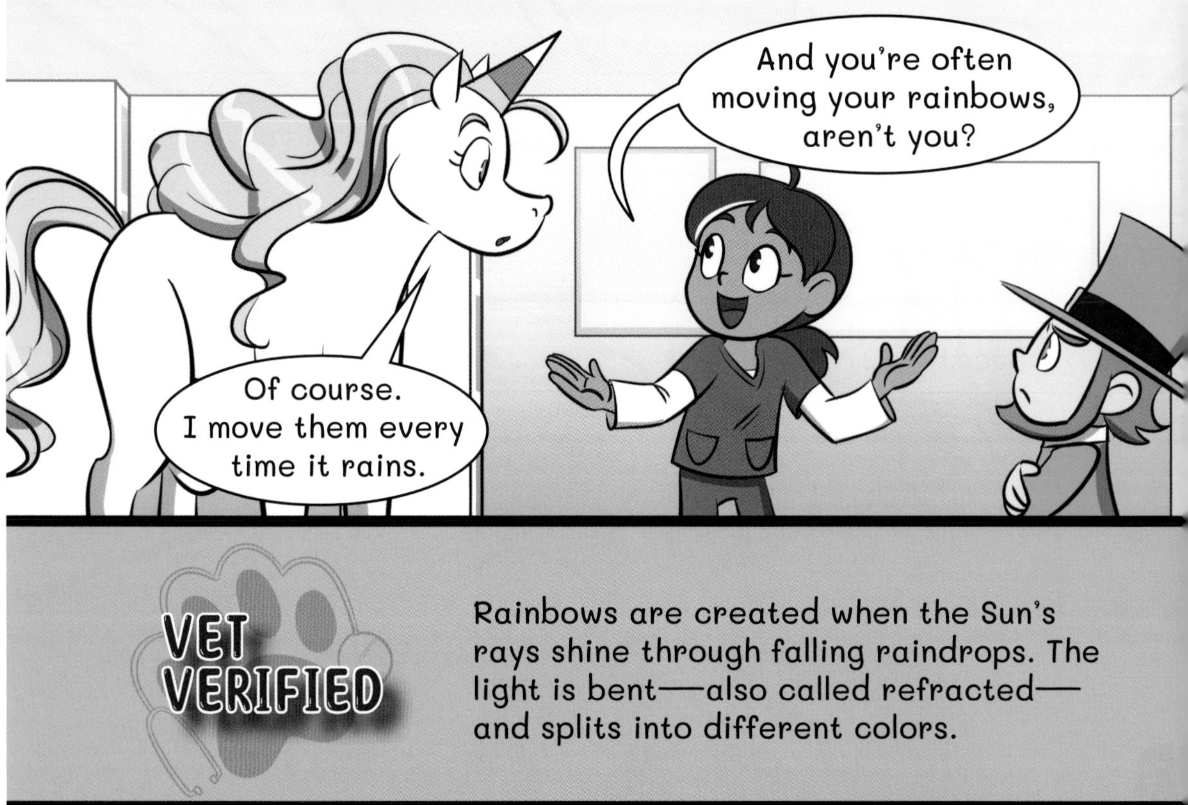
And you're often moving your rainbows, aren't you?
Of course. I move them every time it rains.

VET VERIFIED

Rainbows are created when the Sun's rays shine through falling raindrops. The light is bent—also called refracted—and splits into different colors.

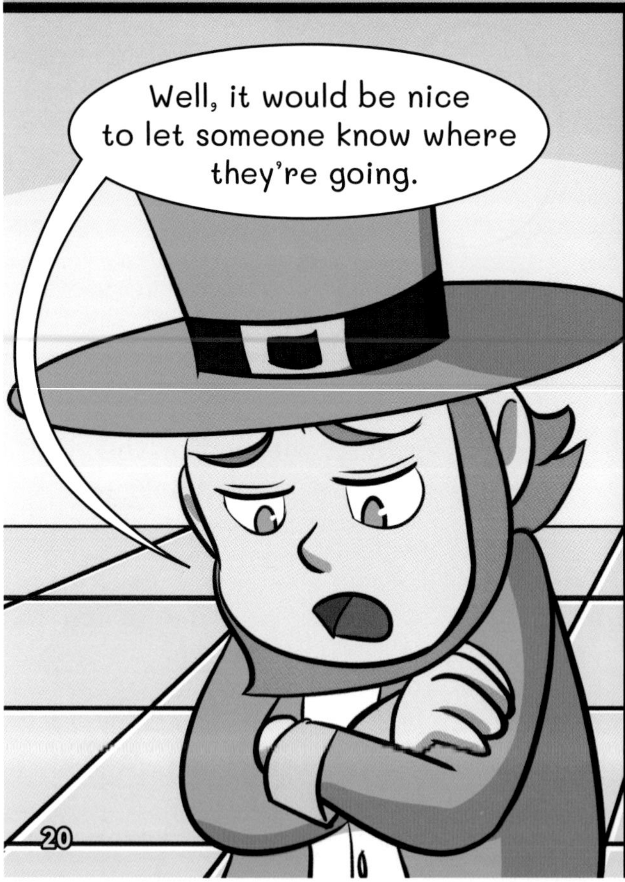
Well, it would be nice to let someone know where they're going.

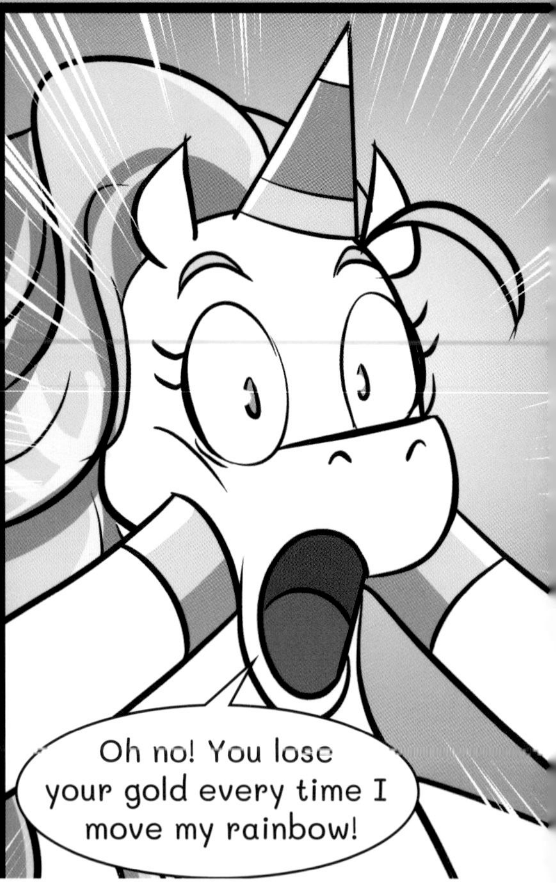
Oh no! You lose your gold every time I move my rainbow!

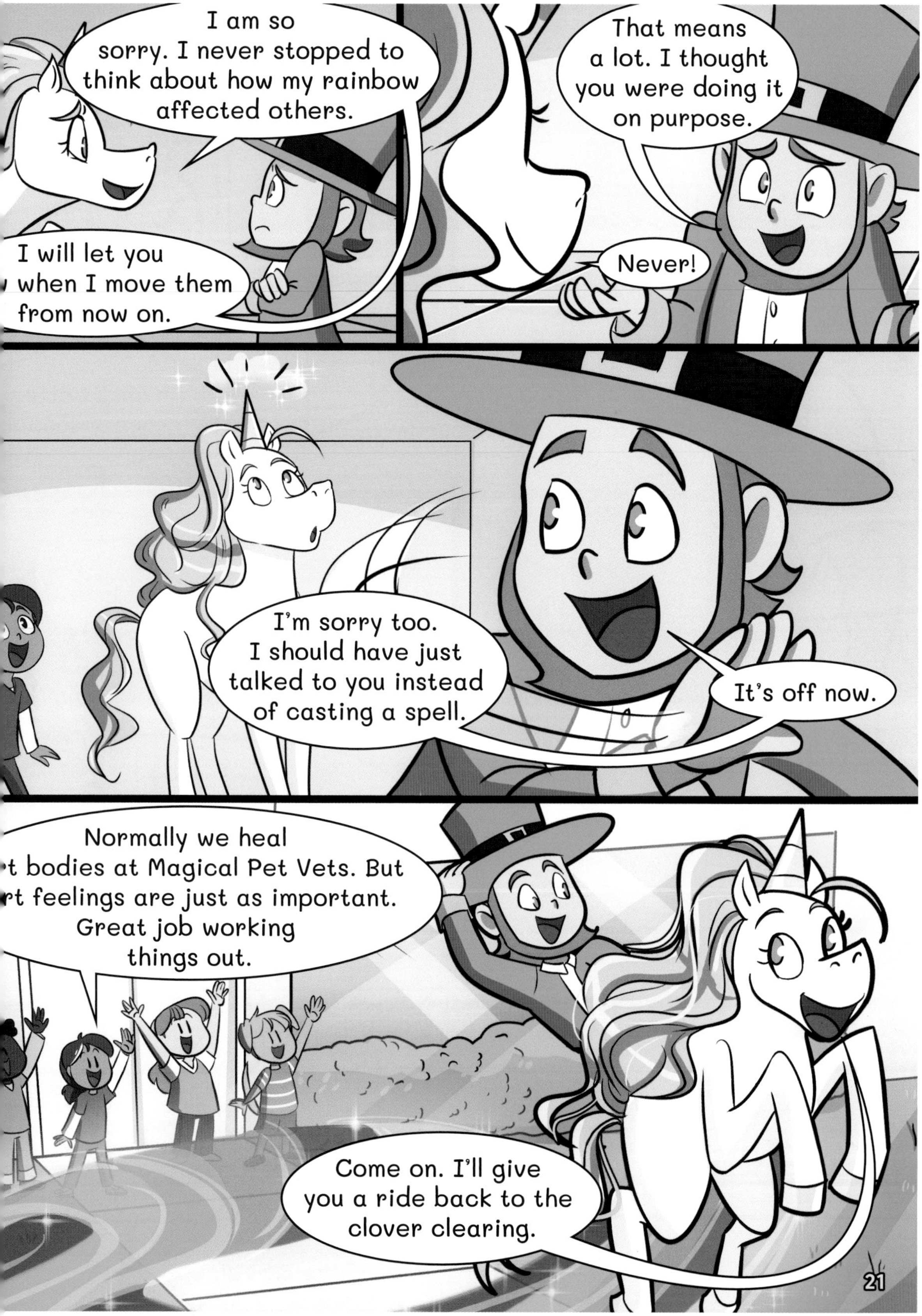

I am so sorry. I never stopped to think about how my rainbow affected others.
I will let you when I move them from now on.
That means a lot. I thought you were doing it on purpose.
Never!
I'm sorry too. I should have just talked to you instead of casting a spell.
It's off now.
Normally we heal t bodies at Magical Pet Vets. But rt feelings are just as important. Great job working things out.
Come on. I'll give you a ride back to the clover clearing.

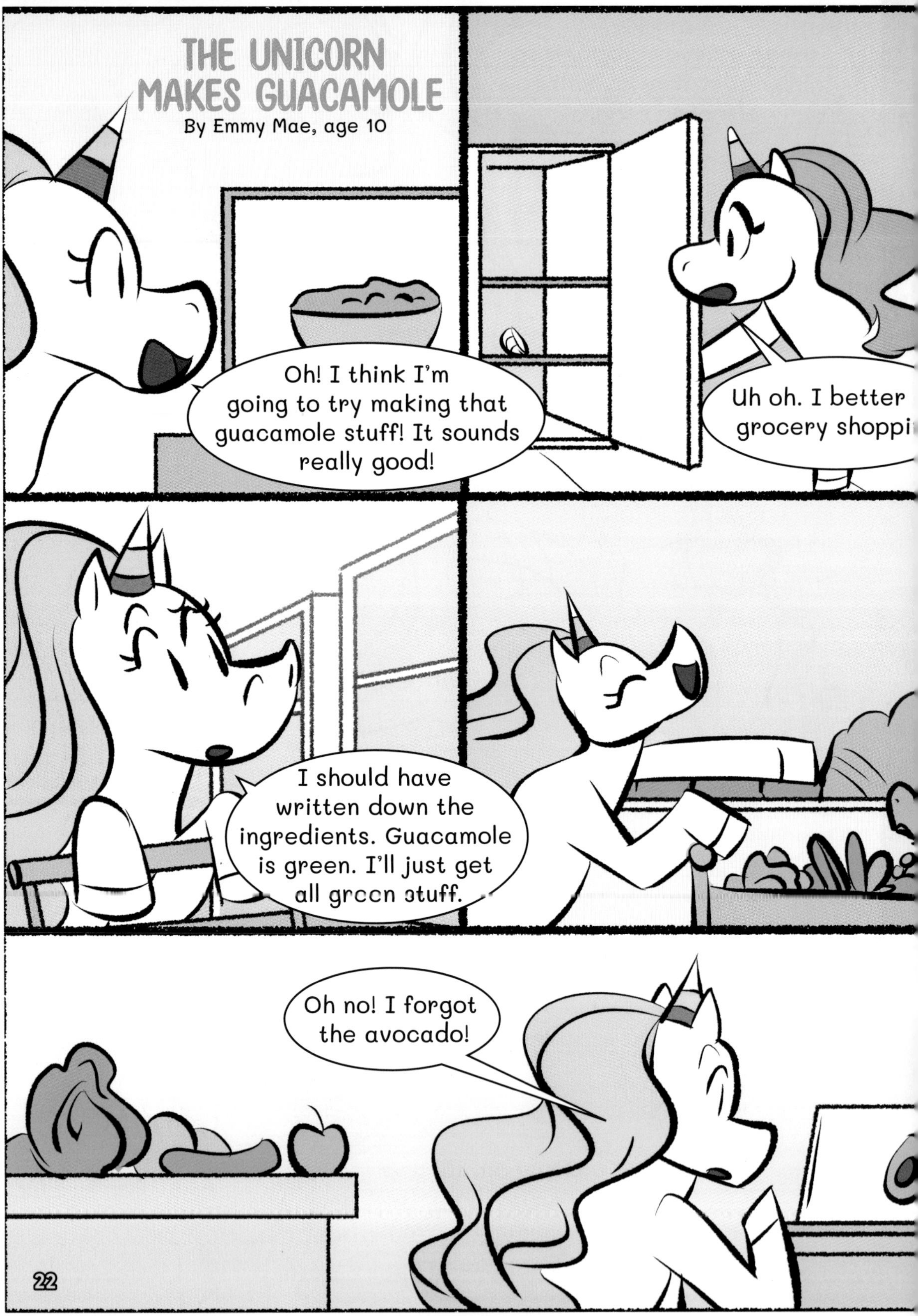
THE UNICORN MAKES GUACAMOLE
By Emmy Mae, age 10
Oh! I think I'm going to try making that guacamole stuff! It sounds really good!
Uh oh. I better grocery shoppi
I should have written down the ingredients. Guacamole is green. I'll just get all green stuff.
Oh no! I forgot the avocado!

LEARN MORE

BOOKS

Drimmer, Stephanie. *Mythical Beasts.* Washington, DC: National Geographic Kids, 2022.

Reeves, Diane Lindsey. *Do You Like Taking Care of Animals?* Ann Arbor, MI: Cherry Lake Publishing, 2023.

EXPLORE THESE ONLINE RESOURCES WITH AN ADULT

Inspiremykids.com - Careers That Count: So You Want to Be a Veterinarian?
By Kristen Blake

Kids Play and Create - Rainbow Facts for Kids and Teachers

BIOS

Emily wants to become a professional football player someday. Until then, she is happy helping out at the Magical Pet Vet. Not only is Marta her best friend, but she has so much fun meeting all of the interesting creatures who come in for help.

Marta has always had a love for animals. Since she could dream, she has wanted to be a veterinarian. When she discovered that there were creatures in her town that not everyone knew about—creatures many people think of as monsters—she opened up the Magical Pet Vet to help them stay healthy and happy.

Taye can create anything with technology. He has always understood machines. After becoming friends with Marta and Emily, he realized he could put his skills to use helping creatures in ways that even a doctor can't.

Glossary

cast (KAST) performed magic

drone (DROHN) an unpiloted, remote-controlled aircraft

leprechaun (LEP-ruh-kahn) a dwarf or elf in Irish folklore that likes to gather and hide treasure

patient (PAY-shunt) someone who gets medical care

residue (REZ-uh-doo) what is left after something burns up or evaporates

spell (SPEL) a word or words supposed to have magical powers

werewolf (WEHR-wulf) a human who turns into a wolf

Index